Valerie Dalton

TOUCHSTONES

A Book
of Simple Truths

ASHGROVE PRESS, BATH

First published in Great Britain by
ASHGROVE PRESS LIMITED
4 Brassmill Centre, Brassmill Lane
Bath, BA1 3JN
and distributed in the USA by
Avery Publishing Group Inc.
120 Old Broadway
Garden City Park
New York 11040

First published 1990

British Library Cataloguing in Publication Data
Dalton, Valerie
Touchstones: A Book of Simple Truths
1. Quotations, to 1977 – Anthologies – English texts
1. Title
808.88'2

ISBN 1-85398-015-3

Photoset by Sulis Typesetting, Bath

Printed and bound in the UK at the Bath Press

Each quotation in this book comes from a source which has, at some time in my life, brought me understanding, direction and always inspiration.

I wish to express my gratitude to the great teachers and writers of these words, and I feel privileged to be able to pass on these messages of hope and healing to all those who seek the truth in their hearts.

It is with a heartfelt thank-you that I dedicate this book to Dr Jan Chisholm and his staff and patients at Grove Road, Barrow and Ham Green Hospitals, and most especially to Andrea Lawton and Pete Barwell.

...Go Beyond yourself.
You will know
who you truly are.

SRI CHINMOY

Let go of all you think you know.
Be honest; all you know
is of the past. It does not exist
in the eyes of God.

In the eyes of God,
your knowledge is but dust
in the eye of a child,
blinding you to the splendour
of Creation.

KEN CAREY

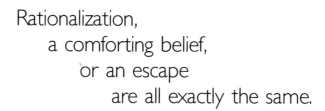

Rationalization,
a comforting belief,
or an escape
are all exactly the same.

KRISHNAMURTI

The way of cowardice
is to embed ourselves in a cocoon,
in which we perpetuate
our habitual patterns.
When we are constantly recreating
our basic patterns
of behaviour and thought,
we never have to leap
into fresh air
or on to fresh ground.

CHÖGYAM TRUNGPA

Whatever you can do, or dream you can,
begin it.
Boldness has genius, power,
and magic in it.

GOETHE

When there is conflict
between the heart and the brain,
let the heart be followed,
because intellect
has only one state, reason,
and within that, intellect works,
and cannot get beyond.

SWAMI VIVEKANANDA

If you shut your door
    to all errors
        truth will be shut out.

RABINDRANATH TAGORE

Stay true
to the voice within you.

This voice is your smartest,
unhurt self
who knows at every juncture
what is best to do

and who does not ever
bend to fear.

CHRISTOPHER SPENCE

Each experiences his humanness

to the degree he can open

to his joy and sorrow.

STEPHEN LEVINE

What we are today
comes from our thoughts
of yesterday, and our
present thoughts build
our life of tomorrow;
our life is the creation
of our mind.
If a man speaks or
acts with a pure mind,
joy follows him as
his own shadow.

DHAMMAPADA

An ill-directed mind
does greater harm to the self
than a hater
does to another hater
or an enemy
to another enemy.

DHAMMAPADA

Let go all the trivial things
that churn and bubble
on the surface of your mind,
and reach down and below them
to the Kingdom of Heaven.

There is a place in you
where there is
perfect peace.

There is a place in you
where nothing is impossible.

There is a place in you
where the strength of God abides.

A COURSE IN MIRACLES

As selfishness and complaint
      pervert and cloud the mind
            so love with its joy
                  clears and sharpens the vision.

HELEN KELLER

When you judge
you go deaf,
blind,
and indifferent

and get stuck
in that moment.

Judgement
is like elastic;

it snaps back
at you.

RESHAD FEILD

When we relate from the heart,
we see a world
of awareness
and effortless activity.

When we relate from the mind,
our perception of the world
is imprisoned
by our preference and thirsts.

STEPHEN LEVINE

Everything that you need
exists in this present moment,
and this moment
is all that exists.

KEN CAREY

Men stumble over the truth
from time to time,
but most pick themselves up
and hurry off
as if nothing
has happened.

SIR WINSTON CHURCHILL

Truth is not a word,
it is not a concept;
it isn't your truth and my truth,
the Christian truth and the Muslim truth.

Truth, like love,
has no nationality,
but to love and to see truth
there must be no hate, no jealousy,
no division and no anger.

KRISHNAMURTI

...beauty and love go together;
and neither love nor beauty
is the product of thought and pleasure.

A mind that is seeking pleasure
doesn't know what it means
to love,
and without love
there is no meditation,
there is no understanding of truth.

KRISHNAMURTI

If you would learn the secret
of right relations,
look only for the divine
in people and things,
and leave all the rest
to God.

J. ALLEN BOONE

Fear of the Will of God
is one of the strangest beliefs
the human mind has ever made.

What seems to be
the fear of God
is really the fear
of your own reality.

A COURSE IN MIRACLES

Beauty is truth, truth beauty;
That is all ye know on earth,
and all ye need to know.

JOHN KEATS

When we no longer cling
to our knowing, but simply
open to the truth of each moment
as it is,
life goes beyond heaven and hell,
beyond the mind's constant angling
for satisfaction.

STEPHEN LEVINE

Trust God implicitly,
and the Truth
of His divine design
will be revealed
in every situation.

KEN CAREY

Wealth may be sacrificed for health,
wealth and health for self-respect,
and all three —
wealth, health and self-respect —
for one's own religion.
But to gain God,
everything — including religion —
should be sacrificed
without hesitation.

MEHER BABA

Desire wants
what it does not have.

Freedom
is the uncovering
of what has always been there.

STEPHEN LEVINE

No faith is our own
that we have not arduously won.

HAVELOCK ELLIS

...something in you dies
when you bear the unbearable.
And it is only
in that dark night of the soul
that you are prepared
to see as God sees
and to love
as God loves.

RAM DASS

If we are truly
in the present moment,

and not being carried away
by our thoughts and fantasies,

then we are in a position
to be free of fate

and available to our destiny.

When we are
in the present moment,

our work on Earth begins.

RESHAD FEILD

...we could never learn to be brave and patient
if there were only joy in the world.

HELEN KELLER

Real fearlessness
is the product of tenderness.
It comes from letting the world
tickle your heart,
your raw and beautiful heart.
You are willing
to open up,
without resistance or shyness,
and face the world.
You are willing
to share your heart
with others.

CHÖGYAM TRUNGPA

Our power is expressed
in the goals we set
and the action we take.

Our goals must express
our fondest dreams,
our commitment
to living without limits,

and the things

which make our hearts sing.

CHRISTOPHER SPENCE

Don't compromise yourself.
You are all you've got.

JANIS JOPLIN

Life is not an emergency.

RAM DASS

What lies behind us, and
what lies before us
are tiny matters,
compared to
what lies
within us.

EMERSON

Lowly understanding of self
is a surer road to God
than a profound seeking
after knowledge.

IMITATION OF CHRIST

Though one were to conquer a million men
in battle,
that man who conquers himself
is the greater victor.

DHAMMAPADA

Even as
a great rock
is not shaken
by the wind,
the wise man
is not shaken
by praise or blame.

DHAMMAPADA

You must do the thing
you think you cannot do.

ELEANOR ROOSEVELT

It is good to have an end
to journey towards;
but it is the journey that matters,
in the end.

Life is either

a daring adventure

or nothing.

HELEN KELLER

How you are
Is all there is,
While you are.

ANON

Act from the heart,
Do not be content
with words;
get to the inner meaning of life,
to the heart of a brother,
to the heart of a group,
to the heart of humanity,
and to the heart of the earth.

Faith is a living
and unshakeable confidence,
a belief in the Grace of God
so assured
that a man
would die a thousand deaths
for its sake.

MARTIN LUTHER

That thou mayest have pleasure in everything
　　seek pleasure in nothing
That thou mayest know everything
　　seek to know nothing
That thou mayest possess all things
　　seek to possess nothing
That thou mayest be everything
　　seek to be nothing.

ST JOHN OF THE CROSS

The author wishes to thank the following for permission to quote material from their books:

AIDS: *Time to Reclaim our Power,* Christopher Spence, Lifestory, London
The Complete Works of Winston S. Churchill, Cassell, London
A Course in Miracles, Arkana, Penguin Books, London
The Dance of Life, Havelock Ellis, Greenwood Press, London
Kinship with all Life, J. Allen Boone, Harper & Row, New York
Man's Eternal Quest, Paramahansa Yogananda, Self-Realization Fellowship, USA
Realization and its Methods, Swami Vivekananda, Ubodhan Office, India
The Sacred Path of the Warrior, Chogyam Trungpa, Shambhala, Boston
Story of my Life, Helen Keller, Collier Macmillan, London
Stray Birds, Rabindranath Tagore, Macmillan, India
Talks in Europe 1968, J. Krishnamurti, Servire, Wassenaar, Netherlands
A Travelling People's Feild Guide, Reshad Feild, Element Books, Shaftesbury

The writings of Meher Baba are published by Sheriar Publishers, USA
The works of Ursula K.Le Guin are published in hardcover in the UK by Gollancz
The White Eagle Trust is in Liss, Hampshire

Other Sources

Complete Poems, John Keats, Penguin, London
Dhammapada, Penguin, London
Imitation of Christ, Thomas a Kempis, Everyman, Dent, London
Portable Emerson, Ralph Waldo Emerson, Penguin, London
Selected Poems, J.W. Von Goethe, Penguin, London
The works of Martin Luther are published by Fortress Publishers, USA

We have made every effort to acknowledge the holders of copyright works. Please advise the publisher of any error or omission in attribution.